And The Books Were Opened

(This is the Second Death)

Timothy White, Sr.

For information contact:
info@uptownmediaventures.com

Book and Cover design by Tim White Publishing

ISBN: 978-1-68121-104-6

10 9 8 7 6 5 4 3 2 1

Table of Contents

Introduction

The word of God seems to confuse so many of its readers, but this should not come as a surprise to us since we know the bible is spiritually based and those who seek the truth in scripture must enter into the Bible on a spiritual level, they must be led by the Spirit, and if so what at first seemed difficult to grasp opens up to them.

The bible was written for the spiritual man, and yes, we are all spiritual beings housed in bodies of flesh, and we were created to be so. We were given fleshly bodies as we live in a world of flesh or tangible things, but man is first and foremost a spiritual being.

We are human spiritual beings who originally were made in the image and likeness of our Creator (Genesis 1: 26), and like most children we tend not to follow or obey the wishes of our parents and go about seeking to do what we want to do, when we want, and how we want to do things, and as a result, we were made in the image and likeness of sinful man, Adam, (Genesis 5: 2).

Our flesh (human desires) and spirit are at constant war with one another (Romans 7), and because of this internal warring there comes disputes, bickering and confusion.

Where there are people, there must be rules, guidelines and even penalties for violating these rules or laws.

Loving parents never force their will on their children, but they warn them that there are consequences for the actions they might take in defiance of their parent's wishes and instructions.

When God breathed into man his breath of life, man became a living soul (Genesis 2: 7), a thinking creation of choice and the ultimate form of life, man was made just a little lower than the angels on the scale of creation (Psalms 8), man was like his Father, his Creator, even given dominion (authority, power) over all that was created before him.

As it is said, with great power comes also great responsibility. God put all the works of his hands under man's authority, The Lord God gave man, (Adam) power over all the earth to subdue (rule) it.

Something happened, (as we will speak of this later) in the course of time, we find man giving up his position and power.

Adam rejects his fathers will, and went about doing what he thought to be right in his own eyes, (mind), and by doing so plunged the world into sin.

Because of Adam's sin, and because of Adam's act of rebellion, God had to take actions to discipline him, but God's love is greater than man's faults, and The Lord had in place "the way" to restore mankind, and there would be rewards as well as consequences for every action of mankind due to his sin rebellion.

Today we have various means of recording the things being done by man, both video and audio, so it should not come as a surprise, or strange that the Bible lets us know that one day all must give an account of themselves before Him of the things done in their bodies (II Corinthians 5: 10).

We are told, the books (records) will be opened (revealed), and will be presented one day, and those who stand before God at the Great White Throne **will hear and learn their sentence for their sins**. In this writing, we will be examining what the books that are opened might be, and what affect they will have on those who hear them read, and the consequences that accompany them.

Jesus said to know the truth and the truth will make you free (John 8: 32).

For therein is the righteousness of God revealed from faith to faith: as it is written, The just shall live by faith.

For the wrath of God is revealed *from heaven against all ungodliness and unrighteousness of men, who hold the truth in unrighteousness;*

Timothy White, Sr.

Because that which may be known of God is manifest in them; for God hath shewed it unto them.

-Romans 1: 17-19

God's Docket

I said in mine heart, God shall judge the righteous and the wicked: for there is a time there for every purpose and for every work.

-Ecclesiastes 3: 17

When we are summoned to appear in the court of the land, it is usually done for one of three reasons, **1**) we might be called as a juror, **2**) it might be as a witness, and **3**) we might be called as the individual being prosecuted. The first two are not the major focus of this book.

The presumed guilty individual, (*in the court system we are presumed guilty, until proven innocent*). This person is added to what is known as a **Court Docket**. A docket is in the legal sense, a list of pending and upcoming court dates dealing with violators breaking and rejecting known laws.

A court session is convened because a particular matter needs to be resolved between opposing disputing parties, with the final word (Judgment) being rendered from the sitting or presiding magistrate or Judge.

The Judge should be someone that is impartial, and fair in their deliberation in the matters set before them. But we know this has not always been the case, as human nature is not often taken into consideration. In other words, feelings and human emotions, often drive the rulings and not necessarily facts.

Men, (and women) can be swayed, paid off, and persuaded to render decision's based on fear, financial gain and intimidation; this is often how the human court system operates, but it's not so with God.

There are a few certainties we can be sure of when we stand in the Court of God, and they are as follows, **1**) God is fair, **2**) God is impartial, and **3**) God is true. He is quoted as saying, **I am the Lord I change not** (Malachi 3: 6), and **I am God and not man**, (Hosea 11: 9) and we will learn that righteous judgment is devoid of emotion, and there is no plea bargaining for those who are on God's docket, and standing before the Great White Throne.

I have been in and out of court many times over the years, sometimes as a character witness, sometimes as a security officer, and on a personal note, even a few times as I fought for the right to have my own children in my life.

Being summoned to court not knowing what the outcome will be can leave a knot in the pit of your stomach, keeping one up all night wondering if the information to be brought out will be true or lies, this is how things are seen, done and played out in the court of human beings, human views, and human opinions.

When they, (the Lost, unrepentant) are called into the court of the Most High God, each of them will know exactly why they are present. Please bear in mind that there are the two separate courtrooms people will be called to, and names on the dockets for each room is very different, as is the time of those appearing in them.

There's a courtroom for the righteous (Judgment seat of Christ) and there's one for the wicked, and the two will not mix one with the other.

On earth, and in this life, good and evil are seen mingling and even seem to fellowship, they can at times appear hard to distinguish one from the other. In a parable given by Jesus, he speaks a sower. The story of the farmer who planted seeds, (wheat) and the evil one, (Satan) came along also, and planted tares (weeds) as well.

The evil ones seeds look very similar to the ones the good Farmer, (representing God), had sown, when the problem was discovered, they, (the servants of God, reapers) asked the Farmer if they should pull the tares up. They were instead instructed to leave them along, and allow them to grow together (side by side), to pull them up would pose a danger, being so close to the wheat, and might cause harm to the good wheat, but in the harvest, (judgment) they would be separated, the wheat would be gathered into the barns, (place of safety) and the tares would be cast into the fire, (place of destruction).

The wheat represents the saints, the children of God, and the tares symbolizes the children of unbelief (Matthew 13: 24-30), and their day on God's docket has been set.

There's a time for everything in life and there's a time for everything in death. As human beings, our focus is more on this side of life, as if there is nothing following it. I believe that's due in part to fear of what is not known or understood. But the bible speaks of an existence that takes place once we have departed from our human bodies. A time when everyone will have to stand and give an account of the things that were done in their bodies, good and evil; *Let us hear the conclusion to the whole matter, fear (reverence, respect) God and keep his commandments (teachings) which is the whole duty of man, for God will bring everything into judgment with every secret work, both good and evil.*

-Ecclesiastes 12: 13, 14

For a few moments let's take a journey back into the past, and the time of man's innocence, before Adam's sin, and where there was nothing man needed or could want (*or so it seemed*).

Eden, a place of paradise, heaven on earth, created by God for man who was placed in it and given dominion (power, rule) over it, who wouldn't be happy or satisfied with such a place, to have everything and want for nothing, what could possibly lure (tempt) someone away from such a thing as this? Was it possibly desire, or craving for more of the unknown?

It was these same desires and cravings that led to the downfall of Lucifer; in fact, it was his act of rebellion that placed him and some angels (now called demons) on the docket of God for future judgment.

Lucifer, now called Satan had one great desire, and that was to be like the most High (Isaiah 14 :12-14), the creation can never be greater than its Creator, but that's the belief that's entertained by those creatures who rebel and continue to do so.

MAN WAS NOT FIRST TO SIN, that was Lucifer and some of the angels, but some people have asked how could angels sin, aren't they spiritual, even divine creatures, my answer is yes, but man is also a spiritual and divine creature as well, both were created by God and both were given free will, neither angels or man were created to sin, (rebel) but both willingly sinned by choice.

God being the ultimate strategist (in human terms), and Omnipotent, had from eternity past prepared for what would be done by the angels as well as man, let's call it **the God Solution,** it was prepared by God before the foundation of the world (I Peter 1: 18-20).

Man's sin could not be resolved by man's hand, God would have to redeem man back to himself. God would have to come in the flesh and do the work man was not and is unable to do.

God was in Christ reconciling (restoring) the world back to himself (II Corinthians 5: 19), for in Christ, dwells all the fullness of the Godhead bodily (Colossians 2: 9).

The Lord placed himself on his own docket. God so loved the world that he gave (sent) his only begotten Son, that whoever believes in him (*his finished work on the cross*) should not perish, but have everlasting life (John 3: 16).

Jesus was put on God's docket, he was to **become sin, who knew no sin** (II Corinthians 5: 21), Jesus was to become the sacrificial Lamb of God who would take away THE SIN of the world (John 1: 29).

Christ would be wounded (killed, die, murdered) for OUR TRANSGRESSIONS (Isaiah 53: 5).

If God spared not his own Son. But delivered him up for us all and for the judgment of sin (Romans 8: 32), how shall we then escape if we neglect (reject) so great a salvation (Hebrews 2: 1-4).

When they (the unbelievers) appear in the court of God, there will be a couple of things they will notice, there will be the angels of God there, there will be the Lamb who was slain for sins, and the Holy Spirit who moved among them, and brought things to their remembrance what the Lord had spoken will also be there (John 16: 13-15), and finally there will be the eternal Father Almighty God.

You and I will have to depend on the Son of God, Jesus, to defend us before the Father, remembering what he said, *for whosoever shall be ashamed of me and of my words, of him shall the Son of man be ashamed, when he shall come in his own glory, and in his Father's, and of the holy angels.*

-Luke 9: 26

Jesus is our mediator the one who stands before God on our behalf (I Timothy 2: 5), Christ is the Saints defense lawyer.

For the saints of God, three of the greatest words ever spoken emanated from the cross of Calvary spoken by Christ when he said, **"IT IS FINISHED"**, the sin that separated man from God had been removed once and for all, the account had been **PAID IN FULL** with the blood of the Lamb of God, Jesus the righteous.

Jesus' resurrection sealed the deal for everyone that believes, all power was given to him (Matthew 28: 18), and those who accepted his work would receive **a pardon for their sins**, as Jesus ever lives to make intercession for the saints (Romans 8: 27).

At the judgment seat of Christ, where the godly saints will appear, God does not see us, (our old lives) as our lives are hidden in Christ, in God (Colossians 3: 3).

Standing before Almighty God in his court for some will not bring fear but faith; it's knowing that our names are written in the Lambs book of life that removes all fear.

So why then will believers have to go before the Lord, why are believers at court?

There is a small matter that must be attended to as each person will have to reconcile as they stand in the presence of God, and for the Dockets to be cleared.

God's docket for the believers must be cleared. The saints of God are standing before the Lord to be rewarded for their service. Not condemned for their sins as they have been washed in the BLOOD OF THE LAMB.

The Charge

And as it is appointed unto man once to die, after this is the judgment.

-Hebrews.9: 27

When anyone is summoned to court, it's to answer charges that they have made against someone else, or to answer charges made against them. It's been said that individuals entering court are presumed innocent until proven guilty. It's a sad fact that in the court of the land it's also possible to be guilty and walk away free.

Justice is supposed to be blind, and fair in the decisions made or rendered, and without prejudice with final rulings and judgment based on the facts presented.

When going to court, we are advised to obtain legal counsel, it's been said that anyone who seeks to defend themselves has a fool for a client. There are all types of attorneys in the world, individuals who are always looking for someone to defend, for the right price of course. For many lawyers, innocence or guilt is not the reason some of them take on cases, it's all about the money they can make.

A decent lawyer, that does not mean honest, can work wonders and have been known to get even the guilty off free or serve little to no time by getting their client what has become known as a SLAP ON THE WRIST CONVICTION.

Here are two words that most people would like to remove from the lexicon of human thinking, **1) Wicked**, and **2) Evil**. If these two words, among many others were not used, human beings wouldn't appear to be so bad.

The new and reformed definition of wicked is this, good, great, terrific, awesome, cool, impressive, and even fantastic. Wicked is no longer considered vial, but very acceptable as a synonym.

Evil on the other hand is seen as criminal, sinful, malicious, immoral, and wicked.

What are the charges being levied against the individuals that will have them stand before the Great and almighty Judge?

It's only one charge that opened the door and made room for many additional charges to be brought against them.

When man (Adam), was created he was given one simple rule to follow, it was clear and concise, The Lord God asked Adam not to eat of the tree in the midst of the Garden, the tree of the knowledge of GOOD AND EVIL (Genesis.2: 17). To keep the word of The Lord would only require one thing on Adam's part, OBEDIENCE.

The only thing Adam had to do was follow a simple directive from God, and that was to keep the covenant (agreement), that was made between them.

The Lord God put everything he created into the hands of Adam, to rule over it and subdue it. Adam had the rights to all the works of God's hands (Genesis.1: 28; Psalms.8: 6). What a great demonstration of love God showed to man.

The Lord gave Adam the world to rule over, but it seems that it was not enough.

It appears that an individual who has everything, all that is left for them is REBELLION, and to have what is not for them. Those who usually have what they call everything, are also most pronged to defy others, developing a mentality that they are in charge of their own lives and their own existence, even desiring that which belongs to someone else.

Adam sinned, and disobeyed the word of the Lord when he ate of the tree he was commanded not to.

Adams rebellion was willful, and by his act he became a sinner, Adam was willfully disobedient, and all evidence shows that **Adam was not tricked into disobedience, he chose to rebel**.

What Adam did not consider was the consequences of his action. Yes, **he heard what the Lord said to him, but he was not listening**, and this is very typical of any child, even today when a parent tells a child something they should not do, that very thing (whatever it might be), becomes the very thing that seems to peak the child's interest most.

Because of Adam's rebellion, and disobedience, it ushered in a time of change and a need for strict guidelines for mankind.

This one sin opened what we called Pandora's box, and in doing so plunged the world as we know it into constant sin and darkness, and we are told *men loved darkness rather than light* (John.3: 19).The charge against Adam would have residual effects.

It was imperative that God dealt with Adam's sin immediately, if not Adam would also take of the tree of life and mankind would remain in sin for eternity (Genesis.3: 21-23).

The Lord God gave Adam and Eve a chance to speak on behalf of themselves, to plead their case before him, to give their side of the events that brought about this scenario. The Lord came down for what I believe was a daily walk with Adam to find that Adam was now hiding from him (*our sinfulness keeps us from walking and standing sinless in the presence of God*).

Adam, **1**) heard the Lord, and **2**) hid from him (Genesis.3: 8-10). People will hear the word of God and do just as Adam did, they will hide from the Lord from fear, PERFECT LOVE CAST OUT FEAR, because fear has torment (I John.4: 18).

Adam is about to be judged for his actions but given a chance to tell the Lord what happened, and why they cannot walk together any longer.

The question before the court was in two parts, first, the Lord questioned Adam and asked, who said you were naked, and second, did you eat of the tree I commanded you not to eat? (Genesis.3:11).

It was time for Adam to stand up and accept responsibility for his actions, to show leadership, but that would not be the case, instead ADAM BLAMES GOD, saying in effect that he would not have sinned but for the woman whom God gave him (3: 12).

Any man worth his weight, knows that a woman cannot and does not make him do something he does not want to do, but she, the woman, is convenient to have around to blame should things go wrong as Adam did.

Adam now stands in the highest court in all eternity, and blames the woman, and God for his actions. Maybe an additional charge against Adam should have been foolishness, but then how many of us have done what Adam has, blamed someone else for our actions?

God did not grant Eve a separate trial, since they were both participants together, they would also be charged accordingly.

God addresses Eve as to her part in the event that brought them before the Lord, and Eve taking a page from the book of her husband, blamed the serpent saying, he beguiled (tricked) her into sinning (3: 13).

Let's for a moment look at the serpent and Eve, the serpent observed Eve, he watched as she examined the tree, not knowing her thoughts (Satan cannot read minds) the serpent watched Eve's actions which echoed her thoughts, she saw that the tree was one **1) good for food**, and that it was two **2) pleasant to the eyes**, and three **3) a tree to be desired to make one wise**, she took of the fruit thereof, and did eat, and gave also unto her husband with her; and he did eat (3: 6).

Eve was tricked because she allowed her emotions to guide her actions.

Adam and Eve would no longer be permitted to remain in the Garden; they would have to leave paradise, the sentence to be carried out immediately once the verdict was heard.

Part of Adams disciplinary sentence would be to till (work), the earth for the rest of his human life, and to one day die and go back to the dust he was created from (3: 17-19).

Since the day man sinned, he has had an appointment with death, and a date set to stand before God to be judged for the things he has done in his body. But what judgment will that be, as there are several judgments to come?

Adam was placed on God's docket for a sin violation, the charge we have seen, recognized, and understand, we know how the verdict came about, was there, and is there a chance that it could be expunged or forgiven?

As God is sovereign, he had already set in motion how he would redeem Adam and the whole world, to in effect expunge Adam's deed, and the only one who could do so would be God himself. The Lord God forgave Adam, but Adam would have to live with the consequences he brought on himself.

In God's court there is one clear charge, all have sinned and come short of his glory (honor).

God is forgiving, but he is also just, and must deal with sin for what it is. It's sin that separated man from God, and sin must be destroyed.

Even in the sentencing phase with Adam The Lord demonstrated mercy, **a promise of future restoration**, a savior would come, who would bruise his (Satan's) head and who would bruise his (Christ) heels (Genesis.3: 14, 15).

One of the most remarkable things about God's love is that he will do exactly what he said he would do, but man also shares a part in this to bring some things into reality, he must accept responsibility for his actions.

It's a daily test, **a self-check** if you will, to determine if our love is genuine, if our love is real then our expectations are not about what God will do but rather how faithful we are, to do what he has asked of us.

We love him because he first showed his love for us.

Adam and Eve stood naked before The Lord God, guilty. They were not maliciously accused of some random act, as an accusation does not mean it is necessarily true, until proven. **They were guilty of**

rebellion, and they were deliberately seeking to cover up their deed by blaming another, and by doing so, added to the sin already in evidence.

Judgments

Judgment One

Sin

Behold the Lamb of God which taketh away the sin of the world.

-John.1: 29

The bible speaks about several types of judgments, but there are five basic types we will talk about here in this chapter.

I will give as brief a description as I can of each of them, and I hope it will help open the scriptures up to you and those who study God's word.

It should be clear by now that every human being will be judged, as all have sinned, but when they will be judged, and how each will be judged will differ, and the place of these judgments will be key to where they will spend eternity.

We will revisit some material already spoken of in this area of judgment with the hope to show how each judgment comes about.

Let's look at the first judgment that takes place and why. Of course, we have to travel back to Eden and Adam.

Consider this, Adam was a child or son of God (Luke.3: 38). Adam was given dominion over the handiwork of God, and was instructed to do one simple thing by his Father, and that was **not to eat of the tree of knowledge of good and evil** (Genesis.2: 16, 17).

The Lord God's command required simple obedience in one area. The whole world was Adam's to rule over, God kept nothing from him, God asked only that Adam obey this one request. There were angels coming and going, the Lord himself visiting them as well, they (Adam and Eve), truly had paradise on earth, but somehow it wasn't enough.

Adam sinned, and he and his wife were cast out of the Garden of Eden and sin was passed on to all mankind, this is called **MAN'S ORIGINAL SIN**.

Sin reigned (had power) from Adam until Christ. Until Christ came man would have to make sacrifices to the Lord as sin atonement, these actions did not take away sin only covered them, **it was man's willing obedience that the Lord was interested in**, later it would be said the Lord was more interested in man's obedience than his sacrifices.

Samuel, speaking to King Saul said, **it is better to obey God's voice than to make sacrifices** (I Samuel.15: 22), and these sacrifices and offerings would be made until the time Christ dies on the cross.

Jesus would be the last sacrificial offering to be made to the Lord for sin.

As John the Baptist saw Jesus approaching him to be baptized, he cried out, *"Behold the Lamb of God which taketh away THE SIN of the world.*

Now, just how does this tie into what Adam did in the Garden? It's simple, the bible tells us that by one man's [Adam's], disobedience many were made sinners, so by the obedience of one, [Christ], shall many be made righteous (Romans.5: 19).

By Christ's obedience to God he restored us back to God; Jesus took away the SIN that disconnected us from the Father, taking away the penalty of sin, and its death sentence for man.

This particular sin (of separation), is a past sin, the only one that is past; it was resolved on the cross when Christ proclaimed, "IT IS FINISHED".

The Law was given to man for him to demonstrate to God his faithfulness, and willing obedience to keep, or at least attempt to keep the law.

Christ was the end of the Law for righteousness to everyone who believes (Romans.10: 4).

Christ redeemed us from the curse of the Law, being made a curse for us; for it is written, *"Cursed is every one that hangeth on a tree."*

-Galatians.3:13

The Law was not bad or evil, it was like a school teacher, it was pointing to something greater that was coming, that being Christ (Galatians.3: 24).

The key here is OBEDIENCE, we are told that Jesus learned obedience (Hebrews.5: 7-9), and he was obedient all the way to the cross.

In the garden of Gethsemane we found Jesus praying that this cup (*of sorrow*), would pass from him, if there was another way to redeem man, but he told his Father, his will be done (Matthew.26: 38-43; Mark.14: 35-37; Luke.22: 41-43), and Jesus was obedient unto death, even the death of (or by) the cross (Philippians.2: 7-9).

Jesus died and took away the SIN of the world, but it must be said also that, that one sin also leads to others, in other words disobedience gave birth to all other sins committed by man.

What is the first thing our children learn to do, it's to say "NO", to disobey, to defy, resist and rebel?

Now look at Christ for a moment, Christ was in a human body, and therefore had the same limitations as all human beings in bodies. He hungered (Matthew.4: 2), his body got tired (John.4: 4-6), he got thirsty (John.4: 7), He slept (Mark.4: 38), Jesus was tempted just like you and I (Matthew.4: 1-10; Luke.4: 1-13) yet he did not sin (Hebrews.4: 15).

Christ came in a fleshly body to demonstrate to us that we too can overcome the temptations to sin in these mortal bodies, but not without God's help through his Holy Spirit. In him (Jesus) resided all of the fullness (power) of the Godhead bodily (Colossians.2: 9).

There is therefore NOW no condemnation (or Judgment) to them which are IN CHRIST JESUS, who walk not after the flesh, but after the Spirit. For the Law of the 'SPIRIT OF LIFE' in Christ Jesus hath made me FREE From the Law of 'Sin and Death.'"

-Romans.8:1, 2

Judgement Two

Rewards

Every man's work shall be made manifest: for the day shall declare it, because it shall be revealed by fire; and the fire shall try every man's work of what sort it is.

If any man's work abide which he hath built thereupon, he shall receive a reward.

If any man's work shall be burned, he shall suffer loss: but he himself shall be saved; yet so as by fire.

-I Corinthians.3:13-15

As we proceed it must be said that **all believers will be judged**, but it will not be for their sins, the sin question for them has been dealt with on the cross.

So, what will they (the saints of God), be judged for? It will be a judgment for rewards only, what they did or did not do in ministry for Christ.

Many works will perish, being works done with wrong motives or for the wrong reason, the works some even believed were to the glory of God but were only done for the benefit of man's eyes.

These works in scripture are called wood, hay, and stubble (I Corinthians.3: 11-13), what will these things be? That will depend on the individual, the ministry, and work they were given by the Lord to complete.

This much is known, the believers are told that if they judged (disciplined) themselves they would not be judged, but when they are judged, it is the Lord chastening them that they not be condemned (judged) with the world (I Corinthians.11: 31, 32).

The Lord already knows we will mess up, but he also gave the saints a way to keep themselves clean, and unspotted from the world, if and when they sinned.

The believers have an advocate, a mediator who stands before God, Jesus Christ the righteous (I John.2: 1), and Christ ever lives to make intercession for the saints (Romans.8: 34).

And when (not if), we sin we can go obediently (and humbly), to God and confess our sins, and God in his faithfulness will forgive us, and cleanse us from all unrighteousness (I John.1: 9).

Our rewards, (for service) are based on our obedience to the Lord, remembering that God does not look on the outward appearance but he looks to the heart (I Samuel.16: 7), God knows the true motives of man, he knows us better than we think we know ourselves.

The Holy Spirit reveals our true nature as it pertains to God's Word, and it is then that we realize that we have all fallen short of the glory of God and are in need of a Savior.

The word of God helps disciple us, as well as disciplines us, and once we become the children of God by being born again, that is **spiritual transformed**, we are placed in the spiritual body of Christ and made ready to share the gospel of our salvation.

As we move in obedience to the Holy Spirit, God thanks us by rewarding us for our love back to him.

Please understand what is said here and I want to make this perfectly clear, **GOD OWES US NOTHING**, but He is merciful, forgiving, and giving.

God our Heavenly Father, like a good parent wants to reward his children for their faithful work in the ministry, and for the fruit they bring forth. Fruit is important so let's examine it for a minute.

The two main fruit are these; first **the fruit of the spirit**, *but the fruit of the Spirit is love, joy, peace,* *longsuffering, gentleness, goodness, faith, Meekness, temperance: against such there is no law.*

-Galatians.5: 22, 23

This is not about acquiring or having one or two of the fruit, as that would be impossible, we have all of these fruit (attributes), as they are part of the ONE HOLY SPIRIT.

When the seed of the Spirit has been planted, He will begin to grow inward fruit in the believer's lives which would also lead to outward fruit being produced as we will discuss.

One of the greatest rewards for a believer is knowing the Holy Spirit lives within them, and is able to guide them into all truth, and that he is able to comfort them. But that is only the first stage if you will, to what God expects from his children.

The second fruit God expects from his children is **the fruit of their labor**. The Lord tells us to go and bring forth fruit, and that that fruit should remain, hear the words of Jesus as he spoke to his disciples, *Ye have not chosen me, but I have chosen you, and ordained you, that ye should go and bring forth fruit, and that your fruit should remain: that whatsoever ye shall ask of the Father in my name, he may give it you.*

- John.15: 16

What type of fruit is Christ referring to in this passage of scripture? That's simple, he's speaking of souls. As believers the focus is on winning lost souls to the Lord, as Jesus himself said, *For the Son of man is come to seek and to saved that which was lost.*

-Luke.19: 10

The mission of the saints is to bring forth fruit, both inwardly and outwardly.

When we stand before Christ, He will reward each of us for our labor in his vineyard of fruit bearing.

Some saints will be very fruitful, some not as much, and sadly some maybe not at all. All they will have is wood, hay, and stubble, all of which are things that will not stand the test of fire.

In the parable of the sower Jesus lets the hearers know that seeds bring forth fruit, or lack fruit depending on the kind of ground they end up in (Matthew.13: 19-23).

It's the responsibility of the saint to plant the seeds, as the Apostle Paul said, one plants, another waters, but its God who gives the increase, in fact Paul goes on to say, *Now he that planteth and he that watereth are one: and every man shall receive his own reward according to his own labour.*

-I Corinthians.3: 8

Why do we sow or share the Gospel in the first place, it's because we don't know what seed planted will take root?

In the morning sow thy seed, and in the evening withhold not thine hand: for thou knowest not whether shall prosper, either this or that, or whether they both shall be alike good.

-Ecclesiastes 11:6

Clearly, we see that the believers, Christians, or Saints labor not for salvation but rather for souls and rewards (*they can also be one in the same*). The rewards will be unexpected not earned or owed.

The body of Christ will not know the true outcome of the seeds they have planted until standing before Christ for rewards.

Now the question becomes, when will we stand before the Lord Jesus Christ for what we have done?

Judgment Seat of Christ

For we must all appear before the judgment seat of Christ; that every one may receive the things done in his body, according to that he hath done, whether it be good or bad.

-II Corinthians.5: 10

Who will stand before the judgment seat of Christ, and when will this take place?

The judgment seat of Christ is part of the first resurrection and will include the church saints (*There are three types of saints, and all of them will take part in the first resurrection, they are 1) Old Testament saints, 2) New Testament saints, and 3) Tribulation saints*).

Our focus here is on the New Testament or **Church saints**, those who have come to know the Lord Jesus Christ and are part of his body making up his Bride.

Those who will stand before the judgment seat of Christ will be Saints (saved by Christ's blood).

Where will this judgment take place, it will take place in the air, the moment we are caught up to meet the Lord in the air. *For Lord will descend from Heaven with a shout, with the voice of the Archangel, and with the trump of God: and the* DEAD IN CHRIST SHALL RISE FIRST*: Then we which are alive and remain shall be caught up together with them in the clouds, to meet the Lord in the air: and so shall we ever be with the Lord.*

-I Thessalonians.4: 16, 17

Remarkably this will all take place in a moment of time, Paul writing to the saints of the Corinthian church, speaking about the resurrection of the dead said these words, *Behold, I shew you a mystery; We shall not all sleep, but we shall all be changed,*

In a moment, in the twinkling of an eye, at the last trump: for the trumpet shall sound, and the dead shall be raised incorruptible, and we shall be changed. For this corruptible must put on incorruption, and this mortal must put on immortality.

-I Corinthians.15: 51-53

As the saints stand before the Judgment Seat of Christ he will be rewarding each for their faithfulness to the work of the ministry, and just like the resurrection of the wicked dead, **everyone must be**

judged for the things done in their bodies, the saints will be given a new and transformed glorified body like the Lord's as they move into Heaven, The Holy of Holies, and into the Throne room and presence of God.

Sins have been dealt with, rewards have been given, and new glorified bodies, for we shall be like Christ for we shall see him as he is (I John.3: 2).

So the believer's rewards will be given to them at the Judgment Seat of Christ, also commonly known as the rapture, **it will not be a judgment for their sins but for their service**, and how they performed the ministry each of them was given in the body of Christ.

There is also a third aspect or element of judgment to come, and it will differ from the first two we have just gone over, in that it is directed to God's chosen people Israel.

Judgment Three

The Jews

Ever since the Lord had chosen Abraham to become the father of Nations, and established his covenant with him (Genesis.17: 3-6), unfortunately his children have continually rebelled against him.

The Jews suffered in bondage in Egypt for over 400 years (Acts.7: 6) and when God sent them a deliverer in the person of Moses, they disputed with him, and rebelled against God (*as Moses was the mediator for God*), yet again.

God in his mercy gave the Jews Commandments to follow and observe, but this again proved impossible for them (Exodus.24: 2-4). And ultimately even demanding of Aaron that a god be made for them, a god they could see and worship, in a golden calf (Exodus.32: 23-25; Acts.7: 39-41).

Israel has a history of rebellion and they were set aside for a moment while God instituted the body of Christ or what is called the church age. The Apostle Paul called it the WILD OLIVE TREE that is grafted in (Romans.11: 16, 17).

It's during the Church age that everyone is the same in the body of Christ, no difference between Jews and Greeks (Gentiles), all are one in the body of Christ (Galatians.3: 27-29).

Some Jews do not accept that Messiah has come yet, and have rejected the church body because of this. The church was a mystery for Israel, and as we will see in this third Judgment the Lord is going to deal with Israel again as a Nation and as his chosen people.

This will only be a diminished version of some of the events that involve Israel's judgment. God who said He is the God of Abraham, Isaac, and Jacob (Exodus.3: 5-7) and promised to make a nation of his seed (Genesis.12: 2). Jacob's name was later changed to Israel (Genesis.32: 27, 28) and his twelve children later became known as tribes, making up the 12 tribes of Israel (Genesis.49), and later to be called the Jewish Nation.

This judgment of the Jews will take place after the tribulation period, the time that will immediately begin the 7 years of tribulation that follows when the Lord takes the church (his Bride) out of the world, this is also known as **the time of Jacobs Trouble** (Jeremiah.30: 4-7).

It will be at this point the Lord will again deal with his people Israel as a nation. There is always a remnant of Jews who believes God (Romans.11: 5), and this remnant would be the example to the Nation of Israel of God's mercy towards his people.

Even as the Lord judged Israel for their sins, his hand of mercy was stretched out still, reserving a remnant.

The entire 11th chapter of Romans reminds the Jews of their status with God from sin to salvation, and because of Israel's continual unbelief the Gentiles were grafted in (Romans.11: 20).

Quick explanation. The Israelites (Jews), were taken captive by the Babylonians (Greeks) in 606 B.C. and have not been a united people since, this is called THE TIME OF THE GENTILES, and it continues and extends until this day, and will not end until the completion of the GREAT TRIBULATION.

It will be during this time of tribulation that the Lord will judge Israel for its sin. God's love for Israel did not diminish because of their sin; God does not lie so he would keep his promise made to Abraham.

Just as God would keep his promise, he would also deal with the sin of his people as well, for God is not a respecter of persons (Acts.10: 34).

When Christ came, we are told he came unto his own (the Jews), and his own received him not (John.1: 11), later even saying, as a mother hen gathered her brood so would he have gathered them (Luke.13: 33-35), but they instead rejected their King, saying they (the Jews) had no king other than Caesar (John.19: 12-15).

Jesus had instructed his disciples in the early part of the ministry to not go into the way (among) the Gentiles but go to the lost sheep of the house of Israel (Matthew.10: 5, 6).

The children of Israel must be judged for their disobedience as a Nation of people. The kingdom that

Christ came to establish with the Jews will be an earthly kingdom, and it will come to be after the tribulation period, to begin what is called the 1000 year reign of Christ.

As Jesus was ascending to Heaven after his resurrection, the disciples stood gazing up at Christ as he vanished from their sight. Angels stood by the disciples asking them, *why stand gazing up to heaven, this same Jesus will likewise return as you see him going up* (Acts.1: 10, 11). The return of Christ will be visual and physical (**also called the Second Advent or coming**).

Before Jesus ascended back to Heaven (*after his resurrection and time teaching his disciples, 40 days*), the question was asked of him by the disciples, when would the kingdom be restored to Israel? Jesus' response was, it was not for them to know that exact time. But, it would take place after the New ministry message (We know as the Gospel), has been preached (Acts.1: 6- 8).

Jesus ascended from the Mt. of Olives, it was a well-known place to the Jews (Matthew 21: 1; 24: 2-4; 26: 30; Mark.14:27; Luke.19: 37; John.8: 1). When Jesus returns (physically), it will be at this same place, and he will judge Israel (Zechariah.14: 3, 4). God's people Israel, will be judged of their sin by their King and rejected Savior.

If God does not spare his own people Israel, who sinned against him, in judgment, what of those who were not Jews?

Judgment Four

The Gentile Nations

When the Son of man shall come in his glory, and all the holy angels with him, then shall he sit upon the throne of his glory:

And before him shall be gathered all nations: and he shall separate them one from another, as a shepherd divideth his sheep from the goats:

And he shall set the sheep on his right hand, but the goats on the left.

Then shall the King say unto them on his right hand, Come, ye blessed of my Father, inherit the kingdom prepared for you from the foundation of the world:

For I was an hungred, and ye gave me meat: I was thirsty, and ye gave me drink: I was a stranger, and ye took me in:

Naked, and ye clothed me: I was sick, and ye visited me: I was in prison, and ye came unto me.

Then shall the righteous answer him, saying, Lord, when saw we thee an hungred, and fed thee? or thirsty, and gave thee drink? Then shall the righteous answer him, saying, Lord, when saw we thee an hungred, and fed thee? or thirsty, and gave thee drink?

When saw we thee a stranger, and took thee in? or naked, and clothed thee?

Or when saw we thee sick, or in prison, and came unto thee?

And the King shall answer and say unto them, Verily I say unto you, Inasmuch as ye have done it unto one of the least of these my brethren, ye have done it unto me.

-Matthew.25: 31-40

We have mentioned the TIME OF THE GENTILES (beginning around 606 B.C.); it's the time when the world is ruled by those who do not favor the Jews or Israel. And it leads to the time of **the anti-God movement** as well as anti-Christ, and the time of THE ANTICHRIST.

We are told that the Jews were always seeking or requiring signs from God of his existence as well as his leading (Mark.8: 11; Matthew.12: 39), where the Greeks (Gentiles) sought wisdom and knowledge apart from God (I Corinthians.1: 21-23). The wisdom gentiles sought, was the wisdom of the world, not the wisdom that comes from God.

There are two emphasis put on this 4th judgment, **1**) Salvation and **2**) service.

This judgment in part will be during the most troubling of times that those who come to know the Lord will endure (during the Tribulation period). They (gentiles), will be called upon to help God's people the Jews, who will be sought by the ANTICHRIST for destruction and extermination.

We mentioned the anti-Christ, in the former case it has to do with the spirit of the anti-Christ. All those who reject Christ and his message of salvation, as well as his coming in the flesh (I John.2: 18-22). It's a mindset feasting on rebellion and disobedience. It's a teaching that there is no God, no heaven, and no salvation.

The world (Gentiles) will agree with this doctrine and deem anything that has to do with God unacceptable.

It will be during the time of tribulation that the person, Antichrist, will have those who accept his teachings to take a mark in their hand or forehead pledging their allegiance to him.

The Antichrist will be opposed to anything having to do with God or godliness, and that would include worshipping Jews (as well as Gentiles who accept Christ as their Savior).

The world will blame the Jews (Israel), for all the problems existing in the world and will seek to destroy them, that is the woman (Israel) who brings forth a man child (Christ) and the faith they represent must be abolished (Revelations.12: 12-14).

It will be during the last half of the tribulation (called Great Tribulation) the last 3 1/2 years of the seven that The Antichrist and those who follow him (the Gentiles) will do all they can to destroy Israel, the Apostle Paul speaks of this calling it, THE FULNESS OF THE GENTILES (Romans.11: 25).

At the Second Advent of Christ, He will return to Mt. Olive and he will then judge the Nations, bear in mind that this is not the Great White Throne Judgment because this judgment is dealing with **living beings** whereas the Great White Throne Judgment is dealing WITH THE DEAD.

As we have spoken of before we say again now, we are here dealing with the third type of saints, THE TRIBULATION SAINTS. Those who will come to know the Lord Jesus Christ during one of the worst times in human history, much like during the time of World War II, as Hitler sought to destroy the Jews. There will be those who will help the Jews even at the cost of their own safety or lives, not understanding that in helping the Jews, they were honoring God.

Notice, in this judgment, how Jesus will divide those being judged as a shepherd does his sheep. The sheep being those who were righteous, and the goats, those who were unrighteous.

So, what we see here is 1) the **Sheep Nations**, 2) the **Goat Nations**, and 3) **the Brethren**. The first two pertain to Gentiles and the third are Jews.

The Nations being judged will be divided into the groups mentioned here for how they interacted with or opposed Christ brethren or fellow Jews.

The sheep will gain access into the millennium kingdom whereas the goats will be sent to Hell, the place prepared for Satan and his angels (Matthew.25: 41), and those in hell will remain there, until the last Judgment to come, which will be the Great White Throne Judgment.

It should be clear from what we have read here that there are two distinct types of sheep spoken of, **1)** The Sheep of Israel, Jesus spoke of telling the disciples to go to the LOST SHEEP of the house of Israel (Matthew.10: 5-7) and **2)** the sheep Christ spoke of also saying, there were many other Sheep that were not of this (The Jewish) fold, that must be brought in (John.10: 16).

When sheep are mentioned in scripture it does not always pertain to the Jews, particularly as we study the New Testament relationship of Christ and the church.

Judgment Five

The Dead

And I saw a great white throne, and him that sat on it, from whose face the earth and the heaven fled away; and there was found no place for them.

And I saw the dead, small and great, stand before God; and the books were opened: and another book was opened, which is the book of life: and the dead were judged out of those things which were written in the books, according to their works.

And the sea gave up the dead which were in it; and death and hell delivered up the dead which were in them: and they were judged every man according to their works.

And death and hell were cast into the lake of fire. This is the second death.

And whosoever was not found written in the book of life was cast into the lake of fire.

-Revelation.20: 11-15

The Final judgment to be ruled on in God's court and the last remaining issue on the docket pertains to those who have not accepted God's Christ, God's Anointed.

There are some who believe there will be a last chance for those standing at the Great White Throne to be saved, that will not be true. Remember what was said a moment ago, it is appointed once to die, after that, the judgment (Hebrews.9: 27)

Everyone was given an opportunity to exercise their faith, either in God or the world. As we have mentioned before and must repeat here again, those who will take part in this judgment are those who are dead, they are dead spiritually, physically and soon will be dead eternally.

Listen to the words spoken by Jesus, *Verily, verily, I say unto you, He that heareth my word, and believeth on him that sent me, hath everlasting life, and shall not come into condemnation; but is passed from death unto life.*

-John.5: 24

It's important to note what Christ says here. Those who believe in God, the person Jesus came representing has, present tense everlasting life and **shall not come into condemnation** (*judgment*), but has passed from death into life.

We already know that those in Hell do not go into Heaven, as was spoken of by Jesus in the book of Luke in the story of the rich man and Lazarus (Luke.16: 26).

We can't pray, or buy anyone out of Hell, they remain there until their judgment day, and that day comes at the Great White Throne.

Look closely at another scripture, it was spoken by the Apostle Paul to the Corinthian saints about the resurrection of believers, *behold, I shew you a mystery; We shall not all sleep, but we shall all be changed,*

In a moment, in the twinkling of an eye, at the last trump: for the trumpet shall sound, and the dead shall be raised incorruptible, and we shall be changed.

For this corruptible must put on incorruption, and this mortal must put on immortality.

So when this corruptible shall have put on incorruption, and this mortal shall have put on immortality, then shall be brought to pass the saying that is written, Death is swallowed up in victory.

O death, where is thy sting? O grave, where is thy victory?

The sting of death is sin; and the strength of sin is the law.

But thanks be to God, which giveth us the victory through our Lord Jesus Christ.

Therefore, my beloved brethren, be ye stedfast, unmoveable, always abounding in the work of the Lord, forasmuch as ye know that your labour is not in vain in the Lord.

-I Corinthians.15: 51- 58

The statement in Corinthians has nothing in common with the words spoken in Revelation 20, here we find Paul speaking of **the dead being raised**

incorruptible and **the mortal putting on immortality**, most importantly he speaks of the believer's **victory over the grave and death**.

So, it becomes abundantly clear that the scene in the book of Revelation has nothing to do with believers, it is the final judgment of all sin and those who committed them.

It will be at the Great White Throne that death and Hell will be judged. That which held the body (death), and that which held the soul (Hell), will be destroyed in this the last and final judgment.

Death and Hell will deliver up those in them and the books will be opened, and another book is opened which is the *Lamb's* book of life.

We have shed some light on what we believe will be the other books in the accompanying chapters, but what of the book of life do we know what that book is?

There are 8 New Testament references concerning the book of life 7 of them in the book of Revelation (3: 5; 13: 8; 17: 8; 20: 12; 20: 15; 21: 27; 22: 19).

Let's look at one that stands out that Jesus spoke of concerning the church that needs to be addressed briefly (Revelations.3: 5).

And unto the angel of the church in Sardis write; These things saith he that hath the seven Spirits of God, and the seven stars; I know thy works, that thou hast a name that thou livest, and art dead.

Be watchful, and strengthen the things which remain, that are ready to die: for I have not found thy works perfect before God.

Remember therefore how thou hast received and heard, and hold fast, and repent. If therefore thou shalt not watch, I will come on thee as a thief, and thou shalt not know what hour I will come upon thee.

Thou hast a few names even in Sardis which have not defiled their garments; and they shall walk with me in white: for they are worthy.

He that overcometh, the same shall be clothed in white raiment; and I will not blot out his name out of the book of life, but I will confess his name before my Father, and before his angels.

He that hath an ear, let him hear what the Spirit saith unto the churches.

-Revelations.3: 1-6

Sardis, one of the seven churches that John was instructed to write this letter to, it was the fifth named of seven, but note particularly what was said of it, it had a name that says it's alive but in fact it was almost completely dead spiritually and their works were not perfect or righteous. It had the appearance of being holy but was not, there were many who started out saying they believed as Christ stated in Matthew 13 concerning the sower and the seed, they were not genuine and their faith false.

Here is Sardis we see a clear picture of that. Sardis was the home of many sinful devices, it was the place of Artemus (Diana a Roman deity), she was the daughter of Zeus and the twin of Apollo's, and she was the goddess of the hunting, the moon and fertility (Sexuality). To say Sardis had a few issue would be to understate it.

This early church was plagued by the Roman or Greek gods and giving duo worship, trying to serve two masters.

There were a few in Sardis that had not stained or defiled their garments (3: 4), and they were commended for their TRUE FAITH and were told they would walk with the Lord in white for they showed they were worthy.

Now let's get to the heart of this letter, Jesus said because of the faithfulness of that few who overcame (believed, repented, and worship the one true God), their names would not be blotted out of the book of life, and he (Jesus) would confess them before the Father (3: 5).

Does this mean that someone who has been saved and confessed Christ can lose their salvation? NO.

What it does tell us is this, there are many who proclaim Christ in word only, and give lip service, but this is not salvation (Matthew.7: 21).

Then what does Jesus mean when he says he will not blot their names out of the book of life?

Some things are so simple we tend to mess them up by trying to add our own reasoning or thoughts to them, when all we have to do is compare spiritual things with spiritual.

Just how is someone blotted out the book of life? First we must understand that we are all at one time in the book of life.

When God breathed into man's nostrils, he became a living soul (Genesis.1: 26), it was at that very moment we are put into the book of life even if we are unaware.

The only way to be removed from the book of life (eternal), is to reject Christ, which is to die unrepentant or unsaved.

Our words and works are writing a book about us.

Jesus said this also, *man shall not live by bread alone, but by every WORD OF GOD* (Luke.4: 4). The seventy disciples Jesus sent out to minister on his behalf, returned to him, and they were rejoicing at the things that took place, and how even the demons were subject (surrendered), to them.

Jesus let them know that was nothing to rejoice over, but rather rejoice that **their names were written in Heaven** (Luke.10: 1-20).

At the final Great White Throne judgment will be all those whose names are not written in the book of life, their names have been blotted out. Not because it was God's choice, it was their own. **God is not willing that any should perish, but all come to repentance** (II Peter.3: 9).

Death and Hell will be thrown into the lake of fire, where Satan, the Beast, and the False Prophet are, as well as all those who rejected God's Savior Jesus the Christ.

The heaven and the earth will pass away, and there will be a New Heaven and a New Earth, and the former things will be no more.

Words

*But I say unto you, that every idle word that men shall speak, they shall give account thereof in the **Day of Judgment**.*

For by thy words thou shalt be justified, and by thy words thou shalt be condemned.

-Matthew.12: 36, 37

So also the tongue is a small thing, but what enormous damage it can do. A great forest can be set on fire by one tiny spark. And the tongue is a flame of fire. It is full of wickedness, and poisons every part of the body. And the tongue is set on fire by hell itself and can turn our whole lives into a blazing flame of destruction and disaster.

Men have trained, or can train, every kind of animal or bird that lives and every kind of reptile and fish, but no human being can tame the tongue. It (the tongue) is always ready to pour out its deadly poison.

Sometimes it praises our heavenly Father, and sometimes it breaks out into curses against men who are made like God.

And so blessing and cursing come pouring out of the same mouth. Dear brothers, surely this is not right!

-James.3: 5-10 *Living Bible*.

Wait a minute, you mean we have to give an account for the words that we say, all of them? I thought it didn't matter what we said, how we said it, or even who we said it to.

Jesus makes it abundantly clear when he said, **EVERY IDLE WORD** that we speak must be accounted for, he also said **out of the abundance of the heart (mind) the mouth speaks** (Matthew.12: 34), so the only thing that flows from our mouths comes from our hearts.

Words are not just words they have power and can lead to either positive or negative actions.

Besides I didn't mean any harm they say, I was just fooling around, I was only kidding when I said those things. We are told that comedy is just truth satirized and made fun of. If we can laugh at it, then it removes the seriousness of some matters, an event or a person.

Words are heart seeds, planted in the lives of someone else by way of our mouths, and when a seed is planted, it will grow. And many of us continue to nurture those negative seeds with negative water (thoughts), yet expect the seeds to grow positively.

God is omnipresent (*Everywhere*) and He knows the intent of our hearts, He knows the real reasons for the things we say and do, even when we attempt to deceive others by what we say. We must bear in mind that the scriptures remind us, that our hearts (minds), are desperately (continuously), wicked (Jeremiah.17: 9), and human beings are very self-serving and selfish.

Words are very powerful and should be used both carefully and wisely, the psalmist wrote, *let the words of my mouth, and the meditation of my heart, be acceptable in thy sight, O Lord, my strength, and my redeemer.* Psalms.19: 14.

There are those who want to believe that it does not matter to God what we say, and that he would rather us be honest about who we are.

What an excuse, God already knows who we are, and the way we are, but it's not about being the same and doing the same things. **God wants us to change**, to become like his Son in word and deeds. But to excuse the way we are, and what we say, is to reject God's word, his way, and his will.

It's possible to talk too much, and to know very little. James brings this to light by letting us know that the tongue can be ruthless, but it's always in control by its owner, the body it is housed in. The bit in the horse's mouth James goes on to say, is controlled by the rider; the horse only goes where it is commanded or led to go by the rider.

The tongue is small James continues, and unruly, even full of deadly poison, words once spoken can never be taken back.

The wicked don't care that their words bring or cause harm, they do what they think is necessary to accomplish their desires. Job spoke these words, *my lips shall not speak wickedness, nor my tongue utter deceit* (Job.27: 4). Was Job in control of what came from his lips and what was spoken from his mouth, absolutely.

Many of us are guilty of not putting a guard on our lips, or not learning to shut up.

Words can lead us to sin and they can keep us from sinning, *thy word have I hid in my heart that I might not sin against thee* Psalms.119:11.

Jesus asked his Father to sanctify the believers with his word, and that his, **God's word is truth** (John.17: 17).

The Apostle Paul instructed the believers in Colossians to *let the word of God dwell in them richly* (Colossians.3: 16) and God's words are not the same as man's words.

One of the many problems God had with Israel was that they were quick to give their word to be obedient, and lip service (Exodus.24: 3). But, they were just as quick to disobey God's word. their sin of disobedience led to their dying in the wilderness, they did not keep their word to God. It's better not to say what you will do concerning the Lord, than to say it, and not do it.

Keep thy foot [be quiet] when thou goest to the house of God, and be more ready to hear, than to give the sacrifice [offering] of fools: for they consider not that they do evil.

Be not rash with thy mouth, and let not thine heart be hasty to utter any thing before God: for God is in heaven, and thou upon earth: therefore let thy words be few.

*For a dream cometh through the multitude of business; and **a fool's voice is known by multitude of words.***

When thou vowest a vow unto God, defer not to pay it; for he hath no pleasure in fools: pay that which thou hast vowed.

Better is it that thou shouldest not vow, than that thou shouldest vow and not pay.

Suffer not thy mouth to cause thy flesh to sin; *neither say thou before the angel, that it was an error: wherefore should God be angry at thy voice, and destroy the work of thine hands?*

-Ecclesiastes.5: 1-6

What if **every word** we ever spoke were written down, how many pages do you think they would make, it's safe to say our words would make a pretty extensive book.

Many of the things we thought were funny would not be funny if repeated in the presence of God, jokes we laughed at would not have the same affect if said in front of the Lord.

There are those who would say if God is keeping track of their words that would be very petty, this is said due to fear, it is said because the things said were negative and hurtful, maybe even vengeful and poisonous, and would we really want to be accountable for our words spoken?

A soft answer (words of kindness) turns away wrath (anger), but grievous (harsh) words stir up strife (Proverbs.15: 1).

Our words will be judged; our words tell others what we believe, they are an extension of our thoughts that later form our actions.

It was Jesus' words that brought many actions against him, one of which was because he said he had the power to forgive sin, and that he was equal to God (Luke.5: 18-23; John.5: 17-19).

Words have ended wars, as well as started them, words have led people to love, and they have caused people to hate, and even murder one another.

As believers we are instructed, *don't use foul or abusive language. Let everything you say be good and helpful, so that your words will be an encouragement to those who hear them.*

Ephesians.4; 29 *New Living Translation*

Those walking in their flesh are quick to say, "I'm not Jesus", or "I'm not perfect", this is done to justify their sinful words or actions. Here is what the word of God teaches. *I am crucified with Christ: nevertheless I live; yet not I, but Christ liveth in me: and the life which I now live in the flesh I live by the faith of the Son of God, who loved me, and gave himself for me.* Galatians.2: 20

Hear the words of Jesus when he said, ***be ye therefore perfect***, *even as your Father which is in heaven is perfect.* Matthew.5: 48

*Let us therefore, as many as **be perfect**, be thus minded: and if in any thing ye be otherwise minded, God shall reveal even this unto you.* Phillipians.3: 15

*And when Abram was ninety years old and nine, the Lord appeared to Abram, and said unto him, I am the Almighty God; walk before me, **and be thou perfect**.* Genesis.17: 1

Is it then possible for us to be perfect in our flesh? What these scriptures let us know is that it is possible, and the Lord means for us to be righteous or holy as God is Holy (Leviticus.11: 45; I Peter.1: 16).

We are spiritually made perfect in Christ, and yes, it is possible for us to be Holy (perfect), in our spirit, as we live in fleshly bodies.

To make excuses for our flesh is not walking and abiding in the spirit, those who live in the flesh will make excuses and attempt to justify their words.

Standing before the Lord in his court, not a single word will be spoken; it will be what's written in the books that will speak volumes for or against us.

In a courtroom there is usually someone who stands on behalf of the accused, even a court appointed representative, but in God's courtroom the accused stands alone, and their only defense will be what is found written in the books concerning them.

Let's be reminded once again that those who will stand at the Great White Throne will not be saints.

The sin question has been removed and dealt with for the believers as their sins have been forgiven in Christ, and they have been washed in his blood.

As the books are opened, for the unrepentant the books will detail all the things they have done in their bodies, and how they had rejected Christ in their lives, by even the words they spoke to themselves and to others. Remember, this judgment is separate from that of the believers; in fact, it will take place after the believers.

Let's look at a parable given by Jesus to help shed some additional light on this matter, and hopefully give a clear picture of this issue.

Planting and harvesting take place at different times, but both has an effect on the one who has done the planting.

In one of the teachings of Christ we learn that there are a number of seeds that are planted. They differ according to the ground they grow in. In the gospel according to Matthew chapter13, we find a parable given by the Lord Jesus Christ, it was most likely given, in part for those who were farmers, as Jesus usually spoke things that pertained to his particular audience, there field, and range of understanding. But the meanings transcends beyond those who were in attendance to reach across time, to you and I for the lesson they teach.

There are a number of issues that are addressed in these parables (*there were five parables given here*) we will not deal with all of them at this time.

The book of Matthew shows the life of Christ in his role as the coming King of Israel, and the promised Messiah. But with any leader or leadership, there are those who reject it, and rebel against it, when it is not what they expect.

Jesus was about to share with his listeners, (including you and I), how important it is to plant the right seeds and examples if they were to gain the best results.

It's important for us to note the types of ground (mentalities), the seeds are planted in, as this will help us see how good and evil works in this world.

We are all subject to influences, good and evil, but it's up to each of us how we respond to them. The parable of the sower and the seed is a clear picture of the power the world has in our lives, and how we should combat these forces.

Let's examine how these subtle influences can bring about expected, as well as unexpected results, when we are not willing to do what is right.

Life is very simple, and can be broken down into two simple patterns of thought. The first being good, and the other evil, but at the heart of anything we say or do is attitude and desire.

Words influence us, and the actions that accompany them. Our words carry no meaning, unless they have actions, as we will discuss in the upcoming chapter.

Words stir us to action if they strike a chord of commonality. God wants us to hear his word, and then take the appropriate spiritual action. To follow our words with works or proof, that not only did we hear the words spoken, but our works demonstrate we were also listening.

Works

Behold I come quickly and my rewards is with me, to give every man according as his work shall be

-Revelation.22: 12

Works are very controversial when it comes to the church and the body of Christ, and it largely depends on who you talk to you will get varying views as to what it means.

Here is a simple fact to consider, everything you and I do is based on, or around works. Our jobs, our sports, our home life, and recreation. Works help define who we are, and what we believe or trust.

Works are measurable, definable actions, and they speak volumes about the person performing them. As you might have noticed I put the chapter "Words" before "Works" and my reason is, that we think and say things before we act on them. Even those things we claim to be impulsive thoughts, that preceded the action.

We have already seen that words are powerful, but words combined with actions define a person's true character.

James writes, *be ye doers of the word not hearers only deceiving your own selves* James.1: 22.

For the greatest impact, words must be accompanied with corresponding actions; it's like that saying many of us have heard, **"actions speak louder than words"**.

Jesus speaking to the Pharisees posed the following question to them*, a certain man had two sons; and he came to the first, and said, Son, go work to day in my vineyard.*

He answered and said, I will not: but afterward he repented, and went.

And he came to the second, and said likewise. And he answered and said, I go, sir: and went not.

Whether of them twain did the will of his father? They say unto him, the first. Jesus saith unto them, Verily I say unto you, that the publicans and the harlots go into the kingdom of God before you. (Matthew.21: 28-31)

What both sons were asked to do was not impossible, nor difficult, but it came down to their attitude and obedience.

Their father made a simple request of them. But he left it in each of their hands to choose what they would do, and **it came down to how much they truly loved their father what action they would take**.

It's becoming extremely rare to find individuals who have a walk and talk that matches, our actions make our words either true or a lie, and not the other way around.

Jesus' ministry was a work ministry and his words only added to the works he was doing, for instance he said, *work while it is yet day, for the night comes when no man can work* (John.9: 4). Words were not going to get the work done, it would require action.

When speaking of the harvest Jesus was said to pray, that the Lord should send more workers, as the harvest was plenteous but the laborers (workers) were few (Matthew.9: 37; Luke.10: 2), of course this would not sit well with the religious conservatives since many of them thought they were doing God's will, but **busy work does not mean Godly work**.

The ministry of Christ revolved around two things, **1**) repentance and **2**) salvation, and everything else would be complimentary to the ministry. It was Jesus' words combined with works that were constantly a thorn in the flesh of his listeners, the religious leaders in particular. We are told, *Jesus spoke as one having authority and not as the Scribes* (Matthew.7: 29).

One of the things that will condemn those at the Great White Throne will be their works, the things they had done in their flesh, and for their flesh.

Works are an important part of Christ ministry. It allows others to see and know what we believe by the things we do.

The entire book of James is about works, James was letting his readers (*the twelve tribes of Israel*), know that faith alone is good but it is not enough, it must be accompanied by proof (works), James saying faith without works is dead (James.2: 20). Faith is action oriented, not just accepting the finished work of Christ, then sitting around waiting for the Lord to return.

Before I go any further, I want to make something very clear, **WORKS DO NOT SAVE US.**

For by grace are you saved through faith and that not of yourselves it is the gift from God, not of works, lest any man should boast. Ephesians.2: 8, 9.

Let's look at another translation for additional clarity, *for it is by free grace (God's unmerited favor) that you are saved (delivered from judgment and made partakers of Christ's salvation) through [your] faith. And this [salvation] is not of yourselves [of your own doing, it came not through your own striving], but it is the gift of God;*

-Ephesians.2: 8 *Amplified Bible*

Imagine yourself drowning, and there is nothing you can do to save yourself, but then someone reaches down into the water right before you drown and lifts you up and to safety, there was nothing done on your part to facilitate this, it was not by your own hard work that it took place, in fact the more you splashed the more exhausted you became, **because of your own efforts**.

Your life was spared simply because someone loved you enough to rescue you, giving you the gift of renewed life; you did nothing to save yourself or deserving, so there is nothing to boast about that you did.

Our works do not save us; it was the work of Christ that brought this about.

Now this brings us to another important point that must be made, there are some who teach that we must continue to work in order to keep our salvation, this is not true.

The word of God teaches us that the moment we are saved we are sealed with the Holy Spirit of promise (Ephesians.1: 13) until the day of redemption (vs.14). Jesus also said that we are in his hand (care) and no one can pluck us out, but then he goes on to say we are also in his Fathers hand, and no one can pluck us from his hand (John.10: 28, 29).

In other words, we can't lose our salvation, but there is something more we should also know, just because we are firmly in Gods hand does not mean we should be idle, in fact as believers we are instructed to WORK OUT OUR OWN SALVATION with fear and trembling (Philippians.2: 12), pay close attention to what it says, it **does not say work for** salvation, because there is nothing we can do that would be good enough for God, but what it does say is, work out our salvation, it's showing we are thankful to the Lord for saving us by sharing our faith with others.

Anyone in Christ considers it all joy to share their faith with others. We love him because he first loved us (I John.4: 19), our works (actions) are based on our love for what Christ has done for us.

Jesus said there are those who think that by doing works (good deeds) even miracles that this would be what pleases God or gains them entrance into Heaven, but Christ lets them the religious leaders and rulers know that theirs, was the wrong kind of works.

The Pharisee were such a people as that, yes, they were religious, and they did keep the letter of the law, but they did not understand the spirit of the law, and how something as simple as the Sabbath was misunderstood.

Jesus said the Sabbath was made for man, not man for the Sabbath (Mark.2: 27), and that it was not sinful to do a good work on the Sabbath (Mark.3: 4; Luke.6: 9)

Not every one that saith unto me, Lord, Lord, shall enter into the kingdom of heaven; but he that doeth the will of my Father which is in heaven. Many will say to me in that day, Lord, Lord, have we not prophesied in thy name? And in thy name have cast out devils? And in thy name done many wonderful works?

And then will I profess unto them, I never knew you: depart from me, ye that work iniquity.

-Matthew.7: 21-23

There are some who believe they can work their way into heaven, or earn access and the right to be there, nothing could be further from the truth. Does not the scripture tell us that all our righteousness (works) are as filthy rags (Isaiah.64: 6). Our works are useless, unless they are in harmony with the will of God.

Jesus said I do always those things that please him (John.8: 29) and I must work the work of him that sent me (John.9: 4). Standing at Lazarus' tomb Jesus said aloud only for the benefit of those standing about, that he thanked the father for always hearing him (John.11: 41, 42).

Jesus was connected with the Father 24/7, just as you and I should be.

Our works will reflect God as we remain close to him. Hear again the words of Christ when he said, *Let your light so shine before men that they see your good works and glorify the Father in Heaven*

-Matthew.5: 16

The good works referred to by Jesus are godly actions; our good works should glorify God.

At the Great White Throne judgment when the books are opened, this book of works will tell the story of what the individual had done throughout the course of their life.

The works that are reflected by those standing at the Great White Throne are the WORKS OF THE FLESH. The Apostle Paul in his letter to the Galatians warns of the nature of the flesh saying, *Now the works of the flesh are manifest, which are these; Adultery, fornication, uncleanness, lasciviousness, Idolatry, witchcraft, hatred, variance, emulations, wrath, strife, seditions, heresies, envyings, murders, drunkenness, revellings, and such like: of the which I tell you before, as I have also told you in time past, that they which do such things shall not inherit the kingdom of God.*

-Galatians.5: 19-21

Another translation put it this way, *It's clear that our flesh entices us into practicing some of its most heinous acts: participating in corrupt sexual relationships, impurity, unbridled lust, idolatry, witchcraft, hatred, arguing, jealousy, anger, selfishness, contentiousness, division, envy of others' good fortune, drunkenness, drunken revelry, and other shameful vices that plague humankind. I told you this clearly before, and I only tell you again so there is no room for confusion: those who give in to these ways will not inherit the kingdom of God.*

-Galatians.5: 19-21 *Voice Bible*

Our ways are not God's ways, nor our thoughts (will), God's will (Isaiah.55: 8).

And the only way we can fulfill God's will is to be filled, indwelled by, and led by his Holy Spirit. Similarly, we are told that if we WALK IN THE SPIRIT, we will not fulfill the works of our flesh (Galatians.5: 16).

The word of God reveals to us, **the god of this world has blinded the minds of those who believe not** (II Corinthians.4: 4). They will make excuses for their sins rather than repent of them, and turn to the Lord. And we know the preaching of the cross has become foolishness to them that are perishing (I Corinthians.1: 18).

Those who stand at the Great White Throne are there **to receive the just wages for their unrepentant sins** and rejection of The Lord's Christ.

Those who do not understand God's righteous judgment are angered by what they read in scripture, some even asking how can God be just and yet condemn anyone to an eternity in Hell?

It is always God's fault even when man chooses for himself what he wants to do with his soul. Good or Evil, God or Satan, it is everyone's **personal choice**.

We are attacked with shows that encourage us to accept witchcraft, and seek after the dead, or we sit around and watch soap operas that tell us it's okay to cheat on our spouses, have affairs, and to seek revenge and that same sex relationships are normal and acceptable. When we know the scripture tells us that a man should not lay with a mankind as he would a womankind (Leviticus.18: 22).

As they (human beings) did not like to retain God in their knowledge, the scripture teaches, *For the wrath of God is revealed from heaven against all ungodliness and unrighteousness of men, who hold the truth in unrighteousness; Because that which may be known of God is manifest in them; for God hath shewed it unto them. For the invisible things of him from the creation of the world are clearly seen, being understood by the things that are made, even his eternal power and Godhead; so that they are without excuse:*

Because that, when they knew God, they glorified him not as God, neither were thankful; but became vain in their imaginations, and their foolish heart was darkened. Professing themselves to be wise, they became fools, And changed the glory of the uncorruptible God into an image made like to corruptible man, and to birds, and fourfooted beasts, and creeping things.

Wherefore God also gave them up to uncleanness through the lusts of their own hearts, to dishonour their own bodies between themselves: Who changed the truth of God into a lie, and worshipped and served the creature more than the Creator, who is blessed for ever. Amen.

For this cause God gave them up unto vile affections: for even their women did change the natural use into that which is against nature: And likewise also the men, leaving the natural use of the woman, burned in their lust one toward another; men with men working that which is unseemly, and receiving in themselves that recompence of their error which was meet. And even as they did not like to retain God in their knowledge, God gave them over to a reprobate mind, to do those things which are not convenient; Being filled with all unrighteousness, fornication, wickedness, covetousness, maliciousness; full of envy, murder, debate, deceit, malignity; whisperers, Backbiters, haters of God, despiteful, proud, boasters, inventors of evil things, disobedient to parents, Without understanding, covenant breakers, without natural affection, implacable, unmerciful: Who knowing the judgment of God, that they which commit such things are worthy of death, not only do the same, but have pleasure in them that do them.

-Romans.1: 18-32

In Galatians, as well as the book of Romans, are listed some of the acts of rebellion (sins) by man, that he attempts to justify in his own eyes by his own standards, and dismissing Gods word.

God did not bring judgment on man but rather left man to his own devices (choices) and the end results are what we find spoken of here and in almost all our cultures around the world today.

Man's sin is destroying the world, God is merely going to Judge a righteous judgment as man stands before him when the books are opened.

The evidence has been mounting and the proof is indisputable and soon the judge will render his decision as to the fate of those who stand accused in his courtroom.

Is there a chance that some of them might have their sentence commuted, that they might be given another chance to change their lives, if they throw themselves on the mercy of the court, seeing that God is a God of mercy? Let's see what will happen next.

The Witnesses

For there are three that bear record in Heaven, The Father, the Word and the Holy Ghost: and these three are one

-I John.5: 7

In the average court there is a need for witnesses, those who can speak to the guilt or innocence of the person being tried, and then it's up to the Judge to render a decision and judgment that will affect that person's freedom, their life, or their death based on the evidence presented.

In the mouth of two or three witnesses let every word be established

-Matthew.18: 16

There are **witnesses for the prosecution** as well as **witnesses for the defense**, there are witnesses that are truthful and there are false witnesses. In this life a defense lawyer, and prosecution attorneys often seek to gain victories, and a name for themselves in the offices they hold.

There are often other hidden agenda's they have, often being friends in the field they practice and not totally concerned with determining the truth.

Today there is no problem with using what is called an informant, a person who usually speaks for the prosecution, often giving negative accounts of the defense's client. These informants are more times than not seedy people and not honest, they are not known for telling the truth. The bible also has a name for them as well, **they are called false witnesses.**

We are not to bear false witnesses against our neighbors (Exodus.20: 16).

A false witness will speak lies, knowingly (Proverbs.6: 19).

False witnesses are known to lie to get what they want, and they are usually paid for their services, the only friend they have is money, and they will sell their services for the right price.

A witness does not always have to be a person, a witness is something that gives proof to, or testifies to a claim, as Abraham did with Abimelech when he gave him some sheep (ewes) as a witness, or proof that the well that was argued over by his servants, and Abraham servants was in fact Abraham's (Genesis.21: 25-30).

This was as valuable as a deed today in writing. There was another type of witness given in Genesis chapter 31 concerning a dispute between Jacob and Laban, because of something Jacob's wife had done (v.30-34). Things were eventually made right between them (vs.36-43), but there was a covenant (agreement) made between them, and a stone was used by Jacob, as a testimony and proof of their agreement (vs.44-55). It was in effect, setting a visual boundary or warning for each of them of the things they had agreed upon. It was much like a keep out, and caution sign of today.

Of course there are the human witnesses of events that might have taken place but was not seen, or possibly twisted, these falsified statements given were done with the intent of bringing harm to the one they are brought against, as in the words of Jesus, *We heard him say, I will destroy this temple that is made with hands, and within three days I will build another made without hands.*

-Mark.14: 58

Of course, that was not what Jesus actually said, *Jesus answered and said unto them, Destroy this temple, and in three days I will raise it up.*

-John.2: 19

A witness is an undeniable proof given by someone, or something as evidence of something that has actually taken place.

A witness is someone who testifies on behalf of another concerning specific events that have taken place. Consider these things as we move forward in our courtroom proceedings.

But what about the dead, will there be a need for a representative of the things someone has done when they have died, and no longer able to give an account of themselves? The answer is yes, everyone will have to give an account of themselves before God, and bear in mind, that this does not mean they will speak on their own behalf.

Those who will stand before the Great White Throne will be condemned by witnesses, but their witnesses will not necessarily be human beings, their witness will be the things they had done and the words they had spoken.

The bible tells us, by your own words you will be justified and by your own words you will be condemned (Matthew.12: 37).

I know this might be a shock to some, but the greatest lies often come from within the court setting, and is done in the hopes that no one really knows the real truth. It's like what Satan said to God concerning

Job, ***Skin for skin***, *yea, all that a man hath will he give for his life* (Job.2: 4), and that could mean he might even lie to save his life.

A man who lives according to his flesh will say and do almost anything to save his life, and that means he would not be above lying to do so.

In God's court there will be no need for calling witnesses together for statements.

Again, let's look at the book of Job, as this was a classic picture of a spiritual courtroom drama being played out.

God is Judge, Satan is prosecutor, and Job is the defender. Job's daily life was on trial. Even if Job didn't know it himself. Satan had a plan, and a goal in mind, and it was a simple one, **Get job to rebel against the will of God.**

Job was a godly man (Job.1: 1), he was a very wealthy man as well (1: 3), and having material things can corrupt someone very easy, Job had things, but the things did not have him so it appeared.

When his children were killed and his lifestyle changed dramatically, he did not waver in faith, but then Satan had another plan that involved Job's health. Satan's thinking was that human beings will do anything to live and historically that has most times been the case but not for everyone.

Satan, man's prosecutor, went to court (second heaven), and pleaded his case seeking permission to cause personal sickness, and grief in Jobs life to prove that Job would turn his anger towards God, given the right circumstances, and blame God for everything negative that has happened in his life.

Satan did not know Job, he couldn't read Job's mind to know what he would or would not do, but he knew how man responded in the past to attacks of a physical nature, that's why he said skin for skin a man will do or give everything, and anything to save his life from death.

Job although sitting on earth, but in the presence of Heaven said, *shall we not receive good at the hand of God, and shall we not receive evil? In all this Job did not sin with his lips* (Job.2: 10).

It's important for us to know that we must all give an account of ourselves to the Lord of the things we say, as the bible tells us **that every idle word that a man speaks** he will have to give an account in the day of judgment (Matthew.12: 36).

Each of us lives our lives in the presence of God, whether we want to admit it or not, and everything we do and say is known by him, and seen by him, *the eyes of the Lord are in every place beholding the evil and the good* (Proverbs.15: 3).

If man can produce devices that can record our every word and action, God who is greater, can also keep a record of the same.

*For God shall bring every **work into judgment**, with every secret thing, whether it be good, or whether it be evil.*

-Ecclesiastes 12:14

The Lord has no need of witnesses in his court, it will be the record of the things done by those who stand in the courtroom that will speak and do all the witnessing.

Those who will unfortunately find themselves standing before the Great White Throne of God will have no one they can call as their witness, and like the rich man who was in hell, they like him, knows there is no hope for them once there, and they know what will take place at this judgment hearing.

Those who stand there know they are condemned; they are there to learn their fate, based on what they had said and done in life.

There is some truth to the saying, "let the works I've done speak for me", as it most certainly will, in that great day of the Lord.

The word of God was given that the world would know of his love and mercy, but it also shows us his anger, not against man, but his sins. God hates sin but loves the sinners, and it is this very reason why he sent his Son to die in our place for sin.

Guilty

Guilty, the one word no one wants to hear coming from the lips of a Judge or jury, it's the one word that changes a life forever.

It's this one word, guilty, that declares, presumably all evidence collected points to the individual (or group) on trial, as being the person(s) that there is no shadow of a doubt that they are the person(s) who committed that deed for which they are about to be punished.

Before we move on it must be said that everyone who has been put on trial, were not guilty of the things being brought against them, there are people who were, and continues to be willing to lie to accomplish what they desire.

Being seen as guilty is not always negative, as we find in the case of Jesus; he was not guilty of doing anything wrong he was guilty of doing what was right.

For instance, Jesus was guilty by man's standards, of doing miracles on the Sabbath day (Matthew 12:10-15) and accused of breaking the Law.

Jesus was guilty of rebuking the Pharisees for their hardness of hearts, (vs.24-45), Jesus was guilty of saying he was the Son of God, and that he and the

Father were one, (John 10: 30, 32, 33). Jesus was being condemned, (found guilty) because of his claim of being the Son of God among many other things.

How does one go about proving someone's innocence or guilt? How's this information gathered, by whom, and is it reliable?

If asked of man one might want to question the source, but in this case of the Great White Throne judgment it has nothing to do with man gathering and comparing witness's testimony.

What will those who will appear at the Great White Throne be guilty of, what crime had they committed, and against whom?

Guilty in some instances means remorseful for something done, the acknowledgment of a wrong executed, but in the majority of cases it comes as a result of being caught and brought to justice for doing something that shouldn't have been done.

Feelings of remorse does not mean repenting, it simply means made aware of an act done.

Let's look at a couple of things that will be in evidence at the Great white Throne Judgment.

I- Reject God

Those who will appear before the Great White Throne will be there for two very specific reasons, 1) being the rejection of **Jesus Christ as the Son of God.**

For God so loved the world that he gave his only begotten Son that whosoever believeth in him should not perish but have everlasting life, For God sent not his Son into the world to condemn the world, but the world through him might be saved (John 3: 16, 17).

Jesus is the Lord's salvation; he came into the world to redeem man, to save him from his sin, and to be the light of the world.

In the very next verse, we are made aware of this, *He that believeth is not condemned, but he that believeth not is condemned already, because he has not believed in the name of the only begotten Son of God* (v.18).

He that believeth on the Son hath everlasting life: and he that believeth not the Son shall not see life; but the wrath of God abideth on him, (John.3: 36).

There is therefore now no condemnation to them which are in Christ Jesus, who walk not according to the flesh, but after the Spirit (Romans.8: 1).

The word "condemnation" means judgment, those who are walking and living by the power of the Holy Spirit are not being judged at the Great white Throne; they received their judgment at the Judgment Seat of Christ.

Jesus came to atone for man's sin (Romans 5: 10-12), to lay down his life in exchange for man (John 10: 15-17), and to take away the sin of the world (John 1: 29).

Man's guilt comes from his willing desire to reject God and godliness, as well as kill (destroy, murder) his representative who was Christ the Lord (Matthew 12: 14; Mark 3: 6; 11: 18).

Why would anyone seek to do such a thing, to reject God? The bible gives us the answer to that as well, because their deeds are evil, and because they (the lost) walk in darkness (John 3: 19).

God was constantly working in the lives of man to redeem him back to himself, and finally sent his Son Jesus Christ who we are told, God was in Christ reconciling the world back to himself (II Corinthians 5: 19).

God simplified things by doing all the work, the only requirement from man would be applying FAITH, to simply believe what God said and what he did for us in the person of his Son Jesus Christ.

Come now, let us reason together, saith the Lord, though your sins be as scarlet, they shall be white as snow, though they be red like crimson they shall be as wool (Isaiah 1: 18). **GUILTY**.

Even as the nations, (Jews, Israel) sins were known in the days of Isaiah, the Lord loved them, warned them, and reached out to them letting them also know what the consequence would be, if they constantly reject his love. Continuing he said, *if ye be willing and obedient ye shall eat the good of the land: but if ye refuse and rebel ye shall be devoured with the sword: for the mouth of the Lord has spoken it* (Isaiah 1: 19, 20).

The Lord has been reasoning with man from the time of his fall in the Garden, and man has only become increasingly eviler and more rebellious. But in spite of this God's hand has always been reaching out to man to help him and to redeem him, **not by force but by love**.

Those standing before the Great White Throne know they were loved, but they rejected that love, so what is Love? GOD IS LOVE, (I John 4: 8).

For the Father judges no man, but he has committed all judgment unto the Son (John 5: 22).

So, the single most important thing anyone can do, is to accept Jesus Christ as their Lord and Savior, and to escape the wrath that is to come, (I Thessalonians 1: 9, 10). To reject Christ is to also reject him (God), who sent him (Christ).

II- Reject God's people

So, what is the proof of those who have rejected the Lord Jesus Christ? It will be seen in **the things they do, say, and their actions towards others.**

Let's remember what the bible teaches us, that no man has seen God at any time the only begotten of the Father has declared him or made him known (John 1: 18).

Scripture also states, *how can we love God whom we have not seen and hate our brother who we see every day* (I John 4: 20).

By this will all men know you are my disciples, if you love one another (John 13: 35).

Loving God without loving others is impossible.

In fact, Jesus said on two commandments rest all others, *Master, which is the great commandment in the law?*

Jesus said unto him, Thou shalt love the Lord thy God with all thy heart, and with all thy soul, and with all thy mind.

This is the first and great commandment.

And the second is like unto it, Thou shalt love thy neighbour as thyself.

On these two commandments hang all the law and the prophets. (Matthew 22: 36-40).

It is the violation of these two simple commandments among others that have these individuals standing in judgment before God.

The rich man was found guilty and was in hell because he did not apply, or comply with the love of God, (Luke 16: 19-25).

The tree will be known by the fruit it bears (Matthew 7: 19, 20), and fruit in this instance is works. It's proof that the tree is what it appears to be. An apple tree should produce apples, and fig trees figs. A fruitless tree is useless.

If a man, (enemy) hungers, feed him, if he is thirsty give him something to drink (Romans 12: 20), this is faith in action. Those who stand before the Great White throne will be there because they rejected God, the people of God, the word of God, and works of God.

One of these works was to take care of God's children, and his little ones meaning old and young alike. We are all children of God by creation (Genesis 1: 26; 2: 7), but we become sons, (and daughters) of God by accepting Jesus as our Lord and Savior (John 1: 12).

We are to then live accordingly, **becoming examples of God's love in Christ towards others.**

Those standing before the Great White Throne did not honor God, they did not treat his children with respect and now must give an account of their actions.

When the books are opened, those being judged, words and works will do all the talking for them. There will be no mediator standing in defense of those on trial at that time.

The bible tells us, *for there is only one God and one mediator between God and man and that is Christ Jesus*

- I Timothy 2: 5

Christ cannot defend those who have denied him and have been ashamed of him before the world and have died in their sins.

Jesus said, *For whosoever shall be ashamed of me and of my words, of him shall the Son of man be ashamed, when he shall come in his own glory, and in his Father's, and of the holy angels.*

-Luke 9: 26

We find that during the tribulation to come when the world will follow after the beast (Antichrist), men will have a chance to help those who are suffering because of Satan's wrath against God and his children and will do nothing.

Jesus lets the guilty know they had every chance to help God's people and others but did not do so willingly, not knowing if they were children of God made no difference, they should have helped others because it was the right thing to do, and not just because of who they were, or might be.

For another example look at what takes place in Matthew's record of the gospel during that time of great tribulation, at its close when the Lord returns, *When the Son of man shall come in his glory, and all the holy angels with him, then shall he sit upon the throne of his glory:*

And before him shall be gathered all nations: and he shall separate them one from another, as a shepherd divideth his sheep from the goats:

And he shall set the sheep on his right hand, but the goats on the left.

Then shall the King say unto them on his right hand, Come, ye blessed of my Father, inherit the kingdom prepared for you from the foundation of the world:

For I was an hungred, and ye gave me meat: I was thirsty, and ye gave me drink: I was a stranger, and ye took me in:

Naked, and ye clothed me: I was sick, and ye visited me: I was in prison, and ye came unto me.

Then shall the righteous answer him, saying, Lord, when saw we thee an hungred, and fed thee? or thirsty, and gave thee drink?

When saw we thee a stranger, and took thee in? or naked, and clothed thee?

Or when saw we thee sick, or in prison, and came unto thee?

And the King shall answer and say unto them, Verily I say unto you, Inasmuch as ye have done it unto one of the least of these my brethren, ye have done it unto me.

Then shall he say also unto them on the left hand, Depart from me, ye cursed, into everlasting fire, prepared for the devil and his angels:

For I was an hungred, and ye gave me no meat: I was thirsty, and ye gave me no drink:

I was a stranger, and ye took me not in: naked, and ye clothed me not: sick, and in prison, and ye visited me not.

Then shall they also answer him, saying, Lord, when saw we thee an hungred, or athirst, or a stranger, or naked, or sick, or in prison, and did not minister unto thee?

Then shall he answer them, saying, Verily I say unto you, Inasmuch as ye did it not to one of the least of these, ye did it not to me.

And these shall go away into everlasting punishment: but the righteous into life eternal.

-Matthew 25: 31-46

Jesus at his return will separate the nations (Gentiles) and people (Jews) to be judged for their works (actions and deeds) towards the Brethren (Jews), and he does so as a shepherd divides his sheep, (representing believers) from goats (representing unbelievers).

The sheep here, being those who were found innocent after the tribulation, and the goats those who were found guilty. And how will they be judged; they will be judged according to their works.

Is this judgment, the Great White Throne judgment, no it's not, but the end result will be the same, those who have rejected Christ will ultimately be cast into the Lake of Fire.

How this differs is seen in, 1) the place it takes place. It will be on earth at the Lord's return, 2) the people being judged are not said to be dead but living (v.31),

3) they are seen as sheep and goats (vs.32, 33), and 4) some will be seen as guilty and some will be seen as innocent, **at the Great White Throne judgment all are guilty.**

This judgment in Matthew chapter 25 takes place at the Second Advent or physical appearance of Christ coming to establish and set up the kingdom promised to Israel, Jesus is here coming as King (v.34, 40).

This much remains consistent throughout the word of God, it will be their works that everyone will be justified, and it will be these same works, that they are condemned (Revelation 22: 12).

Christ is the judge of the quick, (living) and the dead, (Acts 10: 42; I Peter 4: 5), and those who are alive at his second advent, (*physical return*) that have rejected him, must be judged, and those who have died will be judged in their time yet to come at the GREAT WHITE THRONE.

Man's guilt and innocence will always be determined by his relationship towards God by the things he does, his fruit or works will establish who he is, what he believes, and whether or not he had a relationship with Christ.

No one would want to find themselves in the tribulation period of the bible, especially the Great tribulation. But worse than that, is to find themselves standing before the Lord at the Great White Throne Judgment. **The living has a chance to repent, the dead do not.**

For anyone who has ever stood before a judge, they know whether or not they are guilty of whatever they are accused of doing. But what the living are in hopes of is convincing a jury, or Judge, that they have been wrongly accused. The difference is, we can possibly deceive men into believing what might not be true, but with God, who is no respecter of person, is a righteous judge, who judges not according to appearance but judges righteously.

God's love will not allow him to force anyone to love or serve him. So, the things man does will be his own judge; God is simply giving the reward for those deeds done.

Expunged

He that overcometh, the same shall be clothed in white raiment; and I will not blot out his name out of the book of life, but I will confess his name before my Father, and before his angels.

He that hath an ear, let him hear what the Spirit saith unto the churches.

-Revelation 3: 5, 6

What if everything we have ever done could be forgiven, and not only forgiven, but blotted out and forgotten all together, as if they never occurred at all. I think most of us, if not all of us would love that, as I'm likewise sure there are many things in our lives particularly deeds done in our past, that we hope would never see the light of day.

In this time of transparency, and social media, everyone wants to see and know more about everyone else, we live in a time where privacy is all but gone, a time where security is the new fear; it has replaced individual rights to privacy.

We have a hunger to know other people's business, and it fills the airwaves in what is called reality shows. We want to not only know the dirt. But see that dirt as its being done in real time. It's become a TV ratings bonanza, we have become busybodies in other people's matters (**II Thessalonians 3: 11; I Timothy 5: 8-13**), and now we can't get enough, and we crave it like an addict their drugs.

With the advent of more channels (*now more than 2000*) we can enjoy the sins of others brought right into our living rooms and smart phones in living color and surround sound.

How do we justify our viewing of these shows? It's simple, all we have to do is say we only watch them as entertainment, and besides we don't make them. Although that might be true, we are supporting them by watching them, and our watching them tells sponsors this is the kind of programming we like to see more of.

I am not saying all television is bad, but we must be careful of what we allow to come into our homes. Evil does not just come through the door anymore; it can now enter by way of the airwaves and yes even social media as well.

Sin does not have to make itself known blatantly; it comes very subtle now, almost unnoticeable, sin can appear to have a soothing influence, and it's like a kind and gentle friend calling to our emotions, just like the serpent did with Eve in the Garden, and if we can justify our sinful actions, (*as we usually do*), what we are doing is no longer seen as a sin in our eyes.

Is there a need for spiritual expunging? This is a word that might be unfamiliar to many, but in the judicial system it's a term that is well known, and often sought by those who have been found guilty of what is deemed lesser crimes (*other than murder*), and maybe due to what they call extenuating circumstances, the Judge decides the matter should be sealed and expunged, and in some cases, those who have been wrongly accused, have their sentences expunged.

The reason for this is so that the` individual would be given a chance at living what's considered a normal life, without fear that their past would interfere with their remaining a part of society, and their past action (*sin*), would not be made known to others or used against them in the future.

Expunged does not always mean not guilty, in fact, in the majority of cases the opposite is true, it clearly means, the person seeking it has in fact been judged guilty as perpetrating the act they stand accused of, and the evidence, (*sometimes all circumstantial*) backs their decision up. But the court agrees sometimes that the individual involved would be better off, if given a new opportunity at life, because the **infraction done was by age, or ignorance**.

So, what about God's court of justice, does the Lord allow for our deeds to be expunged? Another word for expunged is to be done away with, to destroy, or to blot out.

There are a few scriptures I would like to call our attention to concerning this matter.

Look at what David said in the Psalms, as he was calling out to the Lord about his sin, *Have mercy upon me, O God, according to thy lovingkindness: according unto the multitude of thy tender mercies **blot out my transgressions.***

Wash me thoroughly from mine iniquity, and cleanse me from my sin.

For I acknowledge my transgressions: and my sin is ever before me

-Psalms 51: 1-3

David was pleading with the Lord to forgive his sin, and to blot, (*remove, destroy*) the memory of his transgressions.

In the same Psalm he goes on to ask the Lord to hide his face from his, (*David's*) sin, and to blot out his iniquities (51: 9).

The Lord speaking through Isaiah the prophet to his people often warned them of their ongoing acts of willful sinning against the Lord. They were constantly rebelling, and God would remind them of his love for them, and their lack of love in return.

In spite of their lack of obedience, God loved them because he had chosen them to be his example to the nations around, God even wearied of their actions reminded them that it was he, who **blotted out** their transgressions, for his own sake (Isaiah 43: 25), even as they were undeserving of this act of love.

This was the Lord's way of giving them a chance to show the world that God not only existed, but that he was with Israel, and just as he was Israel's God, he could be their God also, if his chosen people would leave their idols, and false gods behind. And become the worlds example of the love of God.

If my people, (Israel) who are called by my name would humble themselves and pray, and seek my face, and turn from their wicked ways, then will I hear from Heaven, and will forgive their sins, and heal their land, **-II Chronicles 7: 14**

In the Book of Acts Peter and John were going to the temple to pray and saw a man who was cripple, he was outside begging for money from all who were to enter in.

Instead of receiving money from Peter and John he received something much greater and unexpected, a healing. This amazing healing would lead to a message of salvation given by Peter to all that was in attendance, it was a message of repentance, letting them know their sins could be blotted out in Christ (Acts 3:1- 26).

The Apostle Paul writing to the Colossian saints said, how that they were *once being dead in your sins and the uncircumcision of your flesh, hath he quickened together with him, having forgiven you all trespasses;*

Blotting out the handwriting of ordinances that was against us, which was contrary to us, and took it out of the way, nailing it to his cross;

And having spoiled principalities and powers, he made a show of them openly, triumphing over them.

-Colossians 3:13-15

In order for our sins to be forgiven, and destroyed, they would have to be placed on the cross, they are nailed to the Cross with Christ in his death and blotted out. In modern day terminology they were expunged, our *original* sin was done away with that caused our spiritual relationship to suffer. God took the penalty and power of sin out of the way on the cross, by his only begotten Son, the sacrificial lamb of God. **This was not a freedom to sin, but a freedom from sin.**

The promise the Lord God made in the book of Genesis; he keeps also here in the book of Revelation.

Because man was found guilty, did not mean he could not be forgiven or restored, but I have to say this, **God will always do his part, but there is something we must also do**. The scriptures tell us, *and the Spirit and the Bride say, come, and let him that hears say come, and let him that is thirsty come, and WHOSOEVER WILL, LET HIM TAKE OF THE WATER OF LIFE FREELY*

-Revelation 22: 17

We must immediately act *by faith, on* what God has done for us or is asking us to do, for expungement to go into effect.

In their journey through the wilderness, to get to the promised land, the children of Israel were being bitten by serpents, and were dying because of their act of disobedience, of speaking against both God and Moses for not doing more for them as they complained. Many of them were dying, and God instructed Moses to make a fiery serpent, and to put it on a pole, and anyone who was bitten, all they had to do was look up at the serpent of brass, and they would be healed, (**Numbers 21: 5-9**). Those afflicted had to do their part, not just wait on the Lord to do everything for them.

Jesus said, *just as Moses lifted up the serpent in the wilderness so must the Son of man be lifted up* (**John 3: 14**). Just as all who looked up at the brazen serpent were healed, (*forgiven*). In like manner, all who look up to Christ by faith, will also be healed, and their sins would be forgiven, (expunged) and they would receive everlasting life.

Forgiveness is something that takes place in this life, not in the afterlife. Now is the time of our salvation.

Being summoned into court is not something anyone looks forward to. And knowing that you are guilty makes it even more difficult to do so. Our greatest benefit is having the knowledge that we have a lawyer, an advocate, (*defender, supporter, mediator*) with the Father, (**I John 2: 1**) who is familiar with our case and condition. One who is ready to plead our case before THE RIGHTEOUS JUDGE, and not only defends us, but also removes our guilt by his own blood, and presenting us holy before the court.

Final Word

Surely as we live, one day we must also die, when we close our eyes for the last time here on earth, we will step into eternity. For many of us it is the unknown, waiting to see if there is anything following this life or nothing at all.

Those of us who put our trust in the word of God, believe there is a much better place that awaits us, and we live our lives by our faith and not by sight.

I would personally rather live my life believing the bible is true and treat others the way I would like to be treated, and if the Bible is not true, I will have lost nothing.

But on the other hand, what if I lived my life not caring about others, or how they felt about what I said, or my actions. And not once considering what I do, or how it would affect individuals or their families?

What if I filled my storehouse, (*also called a bank account for many of us*), and I had everything this world has to offer. And what if when I died, I learned that everything the Bible said was true. Then I will have lost everything, including my very soul.

Such a story took place in the word of God, It's the parable of the Rich man and Lazarus. *There was a* certain rich man, which was clothed in purple and fine linen, and fared sumptuously every day:

And there was a certain beggar named Lazarus, which was laid at his gate, full of sores,

And desiring to be fed with the crumbs which fell from the rich man's table: moreover the dogs came and licked his sores.

And it came to pass, that the beggar died, and was carried by the angels into Abraham's bosom: the rich man also died, and was buried;

And in hell he lift up his eyes, being in torments, and seeth Abraham afar off, and Lazarus in his bosom.

And he cried and said, Father Abraham, have mercy on me, and send Lazarus, that he may dip the tip of his finger in water, and cool my tongue; for I am tormented in this flame.

But Abraham said, Son, remember that thou in thy lifetime receivedst thy good things, and likewise Lazarus evil things: but now he is comforted, and thou art tormented.

And beside all this, between us and you there is a great gulf fixed: so that they which would pass from hence to you cannot; neither can they pass to us, that would come from thence.

Then he said, I pray thee therefore, father, that thou wouldest send him to my father's house:

For I have five brethren; that he may testify unto them, lest they also come into this place of torment.

Abraham saith unto him, They have Moses and the prophets; let them hear them.

And he said, Nay, father Abraham: but if one went unto them from the dead, they will repent.

And he said unto him, If they hear not Moses and the prophets, neither will they be persuaded, though one rose from the dead.

-Luke 16 :19- 31

Living by the principles of God's word is not evil, or hard to do at all. But like any and almost everything in life, we choose what direction we will take willingly. We could choose to make a difference in this world, and in the world to come, by doing the things the Lord has instructed for us in his word to do. But if we choose not to follow him and reject his word, in the person of Jesus Christ. If so, then one day we will receive a summons to appear before God, IN HIS COURT OF RIGHTEOUS JUDGMENT.

All the evidence has been gathered, provided and evaluated. It's a closed trial presented before only the judge for examination and deliberation, Since the advocate was refused. A ruling will be made, and a verdict rendered.

The books are now closed for some and opened for others, the court proceedings have concluded, and the final word has been spoken, and the ruling stands. Court has now ended.

CASE CLOSED

About the Author

Timothy White Sr. has impacted thousands of people throughout the world as an author, teacher, motivational speaker and minister. Mr. White is on a mission to positively influence millions of people through his work, ministry and writing, which currently exceeds 80+ books covering a plethora of topics including bullying, domestic violence, self-help, history and spirituality.

The Cleveland, Ohio native, a father of five, has overcome many adversities in his life including homelessness and losing his beloved wife to cancer in 1994. Through much heartache and disappointments he discovered a new purpose and passion to use writing as a tool to "plant positive seeds."

Mr. White has developed profound spiritual insight into relationships over the years. Mr. White has written multiple books on the topic of abuse including, In the Ring with Heels On, She's the Boss and Victims of Bullies. Mr. White writes about these and other issues because of the relevance, and prevalence of domestic and other violence. He believes that, "Information plus application equals transformation."

Mr. White is an Evangelist and former pastor. He believes, "God chooses who He uses." He writes, speaks, and ministers to local, national, and international audiences. With an additional 15 new books in the works, Mr. White hopes to give people plenty of "spiritual food" to eat.

White is one of the producers of the documentary "Where's Gina?" about missing children on which he was also narrator.

He is a co-developer of a tech company (Gsys LLC) that brought blindside technology to vehicles that made billions for the industry, saving countless lives.

He is currently co-hosting a radio show, "Healing the Hurt" on WERE 1490am in Cleveland, Ohio on Thursday evenings 8-10 pm with Host, Rev. Brenda Ware-Abrams.

He is currently on the Advisory Board and is a volunteer instructor at the Juvenile Correction centers in Warrensville Heights and Cleveland, Ohio where his book Seven Signs of Success is being taught.

His book Victims of Bullies is, currently, in the City of Cleveland School system to help stop and make aware of solutions to the issue of bullying.

timwhite55@gmail.com   Timwhitepublishing.com

9 781681 211145